USBORNE WORLD WILDLIFE

POLAR WILDLIFE

Kamini Khanduri

Designed by Mary Cartwright
Illustrated by Ian Jackson

Series editor: Felicity Brooks
Scientific consultant: Sheila Anderson
Map illustrations by Aziz Khan

SCHOLASTIC INC.
New York Toronto London Auckland Sydney

Contents

Polar areas

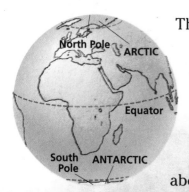

The two polar areas, the Arctic and the Antarctic, are the coldest places on Earth. The temperature hardly ever rises above freezing point so the land and the sea are frozen for most of the year. In summer, the sun never sets. In winter, the sun never rises so it is dark all day and night. Despite this, many kinds of wildlife manage to survive in polar areas. You can find out about some of them in this book.

Strange lights, called auroras, appear in the sky above polar areas.

Ice and snow

It is so cold in polar areas that the snow that falls there does not all melt. The snow that remains is pressed into ice by the next snowfall. Over hundreds of years, a thick layer of ice has built up. In some places, it is about 2 miles (3km) thick. The ice does not stay in one place. As more snow pushes down on it, it moves slowly downhill to the sea. This moving ice is called a glacier.

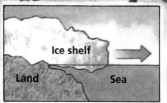

When glaciers reach the sea, they often keep moving outward. They make a platform of ice which floats on the surface of the sea but is still attached to the land. This is called an ice shelf.

In winter, ice forms on the surface of polar seas. This sea ice, or pack ice, is solid enough to walk on. Patches of pack ice, called floes, join together into huge sheets.

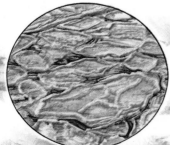

Pancake ice is a kind of pack ice. It is made up of small floes of soft ice. As the floes bump against each other, their edges curl upward, so they look like pancakes (see left).

The Arctic

The Arctic is made up of the Arctic Ocean and the land around it. This land is called the tundra. No trees grow on the tundra because it is so cold and windy, but smaller plants grow there in summer. Many animals live in the Arctic. Snowy owls and Arctic foxes live on the tundra, polar bears live on the pack ice and seals and whales live in the sea. Many birds spend the summer in the Arctic.

This map shows the Arctic from above. You can see the northern parts of the countries around the Arctic Ocean. On maps, an imaginary line called the Arctic Circle surrounds the Arctic area.

The Antarctic

The Antarctic is made up of a continent called Antarctica, the Southern Ocean around it and the islands in the Southern Ocean. The land in the Antarctic is colder than the land in the Arctic because it is closer to the pole. Few plants can grow there and the largest animal that lives on the land is a tiny insect. In the sea, though, there are seals and whales. Many birds, such as penguins, get their food from the sea.

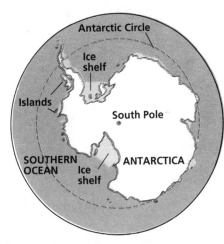

This map shows the Antarctic, with the imaginary line, the Antarctic Circle, around it. Antarctica is one-and-a-half times the size of the USA and nearly 60 times the size of Britain.

Icebergs

Icebergs are formed when chunks of ice break off from glaciers and ice shelves, and float away. Icebergs are all different shapes and can be huge. In 1988, icebergs the size of Belgium were found in the Antarctic. Icebergs gradually break up and melt as they drift into warmer water but even small ones can take two or three years to melt.

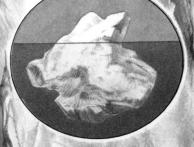

Only the top of an iceberg shows above the surface. Most of it is underwater.

Polar bears

Polar bears live in the Arctic. They are the largest bears in the world - nearly twice as tall as a person and ten times as heavy. Polar bears do not stay in one place. They make long journeys across deep snow and slippery ice, looking for different kinds of food. They eat seals, birds, fish and plants. Adult polar bears spend most of their lives on their own. Baby polar bears are called cubs. They stay with their mother while they are young.

Polar bears spend a lot of time swimming in the icy Arctic Ocean.

Polar bears are kept warm by their thick fur coats and by a layer of fat under their skin. The only parts of their bodies which are not covered in fur are their noses and the pads under their paws.

When cubs are born, they are so tiny, their mother can hide them in between the toes of her front paws. Cubs grow quickly - in one year, they are as big as a person.

Inside the den

Polar bears give birth to their cubs in dens in the snow, to protect them from the cold and wind. The cubs stay in the den for about three months. The mother feeds them with her own milk, but eats nothing herself.

Hole for air

Main chamber

Cubs' chamber

Entrance tunnel

Up to 3 cubs are born at one time.

Some dens have a lower chamber.

After leaving the den, mother and cubs stay together for about two years. She teaches them to hunt, so they can look after themselves.

Bear tracking

Scientists can learn more about how polar bears spend their lives by following, or tracking, their movements. To do this, they put a bear to sleep for a short time and fit it with a collar which has a radio transmitter on it. When the bear wakes up, its movements can be tracked by a satellite in space.

This scientist is putting a radio collar on to a drugged polar bear.

This map shows the movements of one radio-collared bear in Alaska, USA, from 1981 to 1984.

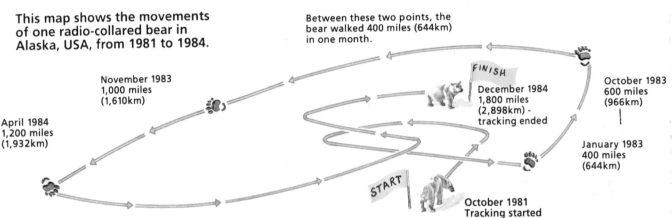

Between these two points, the bear walked 400 miles (644km) in one month.

November 1983
1,000 miles
(1,610km)

FINISH

December 1984
1,800 miles
(2,898km) -
tracking ended

October 1983
600 miles
(966km)

April 1984
1,200 miles
(1,932km)

January 1983
400 miles
(644km)

START

October 1981
Tracking started

Hunting seals

A polar bear's main food is ringed seals. The pictures on the right show how a bear snatches a seal from its breathing hole in the pack ice.

The bear approaches the hole quietly, so the seal does not hear the vibrations of its feet through the ice.

The bear lies in wait, without moving, for up to 4 hours, until a seal's head pokes out of the hole.

The bear quickly kills the seal, using its paws and teeth. It then pulls it out of the water and eats it.

Bears in town

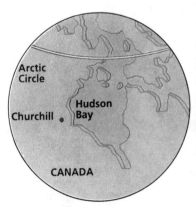

Arctic Circle

Hudson Bay

Churchill

CANADA

On their journeys, some polar bears pass near a town called Churchill, in Canada. They search for food at a garbage dump outside the town and sometimes go right into town. Schoolchildren in Churchill have lessons in bear safety.

The dump is dangerous for bears. They may eat harmful garbage or choke on bits of plastic.

5

Living in polar seas

In polar areas, there is more wildlife living in the sea than on the land. It is hard to survive on the land because it is so cold and windy. Polar seas are cold too, but there is no wind underwater and the temperature does not change much. On these pages, you can see some of the plants and animals which live in the Southern Ocean, around Antarctica.

In winter, the surface of the Southern Ocean is covered by a layer of pack ice. This ice may be as thick as 10ft (about 3m). Pack ice moves around as the water beneath it moves. It is also blown by the wind.

Plankton

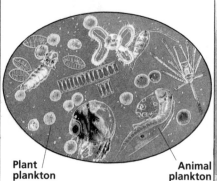

Plant plankton   Animal plankton

Plankton are tiny plants and animals found in all seas. They are very important because so many larger animals, from small fish to huge whales, feed on them. Plankton float near the surface because the plants need sunlight to grow.

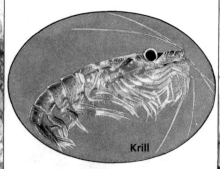

Krill

Krill are a type of animal plankton. Huge numbers live in the Southern Ocean. If all the krill in the world were put together, they would weigh more than all the people.

On the sea-bed

In shallow parts of polar seas, the ice on the surface scrapes against the sea-bed as the tide rises and falls. This makes it hard for animals to live there. In deeper water, the ice does not reach the bottom, so many animals live on the sea-bed. They feed on each other, or on dead plankton which falls from above.

Anemone

Starfish

Sponge

Sea slug

Sea spider

Sea urchin

Sea cucumber

Unusual fish

Some Antarctic fish have special ways of surviving in very cold water.

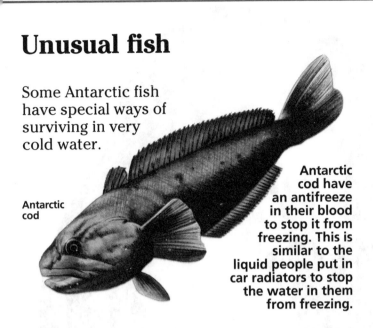

Antarctic cod

Antarctic cod have an antifreeze in their blood to stop it from freezing. This is similar to the liquid people put in car radiators to stop the water in them from freezing.

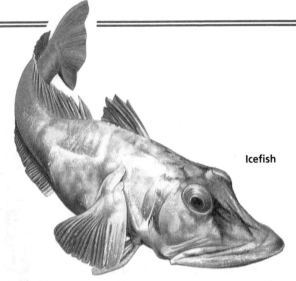

Icefish

Icefish have no red blood cells. Most animals need these red cells because they carry extra oxygen around their bodies. In very cold water, blood can carry enough oxygen without the red cells.

Underwater food web

Wherever they live, animals depend on plants, or on other animals, for food. One way of showing who eats what is by a food web. This picture shows an Antarctic underwater food web. (The pictures are not to scale.)

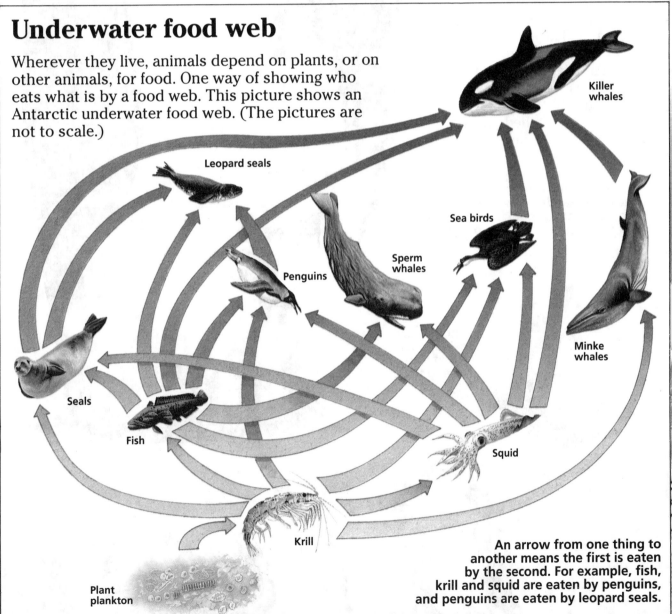

Killer whales

Leopard seals

Sea birds

Sperm whales

Penguins

Minke whales

Seals

Fish

Squid

Krill

Plant plankton

An arrow from one thing to another means the first is eaten by the second. For example, fish, krill and squid are eaten by penguins, and penguins are eaten by leopard seals.

Penguins

Penguins are sea birds which cannot fly. They all live in the southern half of the world and seven species live in the Antarctic (see below). Penguins are kept warm by two layers of short, tightly-packed feathers and by a layer of fat under their skin.

Although they cannot fly, penguins are very good swimmers and divers. They use their stiff, narrow wings as flippers in the water. Antarctic penguins spend most of their lives swimming in the icy Southern Ocean, catching fish, squid and krill.

Penguins only leave the sea at breeding times. They come on to land, or ice, and make their way to their breeding places, which are called rookeries. Year after year, penguins return to the rookery where they were hatched. They often return to the same mate, too.

This emperor penguin is keeping its chick warm. The chick stands on its parent's feet and snuggles under a special flap of skin. Both males and females have this flap of skin.

Penguins use their special flap of skin to keep their eggs warm.

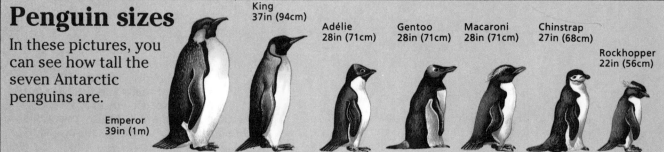

Penguin sizes

In these pictures, you can see how tall the seven Antarctic penguins are.

Emperor
39in (1m)

King
37in (94cm)

Adélie
28in (71cm)

Gentoo
28in (71cm)

Macaroni
28in (71cm)

Chinstrap
27in (68cm)

Rockhopper
22in (56cm)

Ice-breeding emperors

Most birds breed in summer. Emperor penguins breed in winter on the cold, windy pack ice around Antarctica. These pictures show what happens.

South Pole

ANTARCTICA

Penguins' paths

The penguins leave the water and walk across the ice to their rookeries - a journey of up to 100 miles (160km).

On sloping ground, penguins toboggan along on their fronts, pushing themselves forward with their flippers.

At the rookery, penguins pair up and mate. Each female lays 1 egg, passes it to the male and goes back to the sea to feed.

For up to 9 weeks, the male keeps the egg warm on his feet. He does not eat at all during this time so he gets very thin.

Groups of males huddle together for warmth, with their backs to the wind. They take turns on the outside.

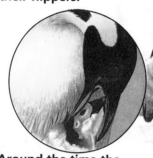

Around the time the chick hatches, the female returns with food. The chick reaches inside her beak to feed.

Older chicks stand in groups, called crèches. Their parents feed them all winter. Then they look after themselves.

Crested penguins

Crested penguins are very fierce. They get their name because they have spiky, golden feathers above their eyes. These feathers are especially bright when the penguins are courting (looking for mates). There are two kinds of crested penguins living in the Antarctic - macaronis and rockhoppers.

These macaroni penguins are doing a courtship dance. A male and female stand on their nest, calling to each other and waving their heads.

Macaroni penguins

Rockhopper penguins

Rockhopper penguin's head

Rockhopper penguins hop from rock to rock as they move up and down the steep cliffs above the sea where they make their nests.

Penguin nests

Penguins have very little nest-building material because so few plants grow in Antarctica. King and emperor penguins do not make nests at all. They lay their eggs on bare ground or ice. Other Antarctic penguins make nests by scraping a shallow hole in the ground and filling it with pebbles.

When a pair of Adélie penguins meet at their nest, they do a courtship dance before mating. They stand face to face, stretch their heads and necks upward and make loud, squawking calls. They beat their wings up and down slowly.

To keep their eggs warm, male and female Adélies take turns on the nest. When the pair change places, they often gather more pebbles to add to the nest.

Adélie penguins

Expert swimmers

Penguins often look clumsy when they are walking on land. In water, though, they are very graceful. They almost fly through the water and can stay under for up to 18 minutes.

Penguins jump or dive into the sea from ledges or cliffs.

Penguins swim fast underwater. They steer with their feet and tails and catch fish, squid and krill with their beaks.

Penguins often come flying out of the water to take a breath. They travel through the air at speeds of up to 16mph (25kph).

Sometimes, penguins swim slowly along on the surface, with their necks sticking up, like ducks or geese.

Leopard seal dangers

One of the greatest dangers to penguins is being caught by a leopard seal. These seals eat all kinds of penguins, but Adélies are their main food. These pictures show how a leopard seal catches an Adélie penguin in the water.

The leopard seal lies in wait in the water, hiding underneath a ledge of ice which juts out over the surface of the sea.

Adélie penguins gather on the ledge, on their way to feed in the sea. Those at the front start to jump into the water.

The leopard seal immediately darts out from its hiding place and grabs one of the penguins from behind.

The other penguins escape by swimming away, or by leaping out of the water, back to the safety of the ledge.

Following the sun

Scientists believe that Adélie penguins use the sun to help them find their rookeries. In an experiment, they moved a group of penguins 930 miles (1,500km) from their rookery and then followed their movements as the penguins tried to find their way back. The map on the right shows what happened.

Penguins started here. They set off in the wrong direction.

START

Sun came out - penguins walked in the right direction

To the rookeries

Sun came out again

Sun disappeared. Penguins lost sense of direction.

Route of penguins while sun was behind clouds.

Route of penguins while sun was shining.

Crowded rookeries

Rookeries are dirty, noisy places. Thousands of squawking, pecking penguins gather there at breeding times. Despite the crowds, each penguin knows its own mate or chick by calling to them, and by recognizing their answering call.

Adult king penguin

King penguin chick

This king penguin chick is turning into an adult. It is losing its fluffy, baby feathers and growing adult ones.

Land mammals

Mammals are animals which give birth to live babies, instead of laying eggs. Baby mammals feed on their mother's milk. Most mammals have hair or fur on their bodies. There are no land mammals in the Antarctic. On the next four pages, you can see some of the land mammals which live in the Arctic.

Caribou

Caribou are a type of deer. Reindeer are closely related to caribou. They eat plants, such as lichens (see page 28). In winter, caribou live in forests on the edge of the Arctic. In spring, huge groups travel up to 620 miles (1,000km) north, to spend the summer feeding on the tundra. These journeys in search of food are called migrations.

A line of migrating caribou may stretch for 186 miles (300km). Caribou are strong swimmers so they can cross the rivers along their routes.

Caribou lose their antlers once a year and grow new ones. Caribou and reindeer are the only species of deer in which females, as well as males, have antlers.

Caribou can walk on deep snow because their wide hooves are fringed with fur, like snow-shoes.

Musk oxen

Musk oxen are related to goats. They live in the Arctic all year long, kept warm by their thick, shaggy fur coats. Musk oxen look clumsy, but, like goats, they are very sure-footed.

When they are in danger of being attacked by wolves, groups of musk oxen often huddle together in a line, with their fierce-looking horns facing the enemy.

Caribou use the same migration routes every year. In Alaska, USA, an oil pipeline has been laid across these routes. The pipeline is raised above the ground, so the caribou can walk under it.

Oil pipeline

Wolves

Top of the order

Bottom of the order

Wolves live in groups, called packs, of up to 20 members. Each wolf has its place in the pack's order of importance. You can tell how important a wolf is by the way it behaves, and by its body shape. The pictures on the right show how wolves stand in different ways, depending on their place in the order. You can see dogs doing this too.

Arctic wolves eat mainly caribou and young musk oxen. These pictures (seen from above) show a pack of wolves catching a caribou.

A pack of 4 wolves has spotted a mother caribou and her baby. The wolves line up, ready to start the chase.

The wolves move forward. Each takes a different path so the caribou are surrounded. The caribou panic and begin to run.

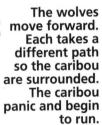

As the wolves move in closer, the baby caribou runs the wrong way and gets caught. The mother manages to escape.

Changing coats

Many Arctic animals have different coats in different seasons. In winter, their coats are white, so they are less easily seen against the snow. In summer, when the snow has melted, their coats are brown or grey, so they blend with rocks and plants.

Snowshoe hare in winter coat

Snowshoe hare in summer coat

Two kinds of hares live in the Arctic - snowshoe hares and Arctic hares. Hares can run very fast. They eat plants.

Stoat in winter coat

Stoat in summer coat

Stoats are very fierce. They eat birds and small mammals, such as lemmings (see below). The tip of a stoat's tail is always black. Stoats in their winter coats are called ermines.

Arctic fox in summer coat

Arctic fox in winter coat

Arctic foxes eat hares, stoats, birds and lemmings. They have smaller ears and less pointed noses than red foxes.

Lemmings

Norway lemming

Lemmings are small, plant-eating mammals. In winter, they live in burrows in the snow, sheltered from the cold and wind. They feed on plants which grow up through the soil. Lemmings are eaten by many other Arctic animals. When they are inside their burrows, they are out of sight, but some of their enemies still have ways of catching them.

Arctic foxes can sniff out lemmings in their burrows. This Arctic fox is rising up on its back paws, before crashing down, front paws first, through the snow on top of a burrow.

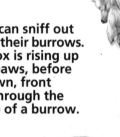

Lemmings in snow burrow

Stoats can fit down lemming burrows. They chase lemmings into their burrows and kill them by biting their necks.

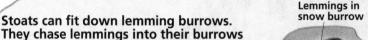

Footprints in the snow

Different animals make different footprints in the snow. The line of footprints an animal leaves is called its trail. Here are the snow trails of three Arctic animals.

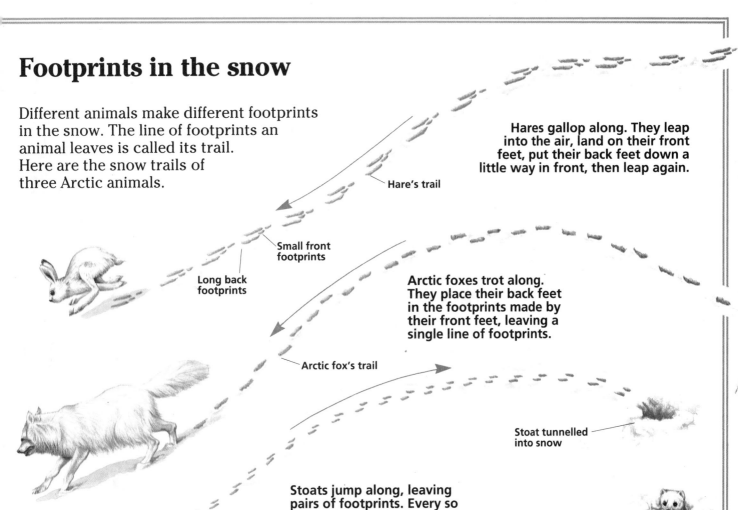

Hares gallop along. They leap into the air, land on their front feet, put their back feet down a little way in front, then leap again.

Hare's trail

Small front footprints

Long back footprints

Arctic foxes trot along. They place their back feet in the footprints made by their front feet, leaving a single line of footprints.

Arctic fox's trail

Stoat tunnelled into snow

Stoats jump along, leaving pairs of footprints. Every so often, they suddenly tunnel down into the snow to hunt small burrowing animals, such as lemmings.

Stoat comes out of tunnel

Stoat's trail

Lemming migrations

Lemmings give birth to up to eight babies every five weeks, so the number of lemmings in one area can grow very fast. When numbers get high, thousands of lemmings migrate to other areas, to find food. Many drown by running into rivers or lakes. These pictures show how the number of lemmings in an area can change over four years.

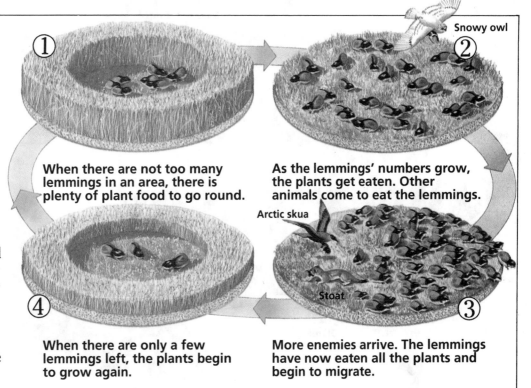

Snowy owl

Arctic skua

Stoat

When there are not too many lemmings in an area, there is plenty of plant food to go round.

As the lemmings' numbers grow, the plants get eaten. Other animals come to eat the lemmings.

When there are only a few lemmings left, the plants begin to grow again.

More enemies arrive. The lemmings have now eaten all the plants and begin to migrate.

Whales

Whales are mammals which spend all their lives in the sea. There are nearly 80 different species. Many of the larger species swim long distances from one ocean to another. There are two main types of whales - baleen whales and toothed whales. They eat different sorts of food.

Baleen whales

Baleen whales eat krill (see page 6). Instead of teeth, they have fringes of tough skin, called baleen, which hang down inside their mouths. The two small pictures on the right show how most baleen whales feed.

Whale's mouth open

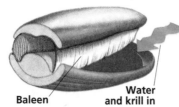

Baleen

Water and krill in

The whale opens its mouth and takes a huge gulp of water. The water is full of krill.

Whale's mouth closed

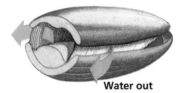

Water out

When the whale closes its mouth, it sieves out the water through its baleen. The krill stays behind.

Minke whale

There are still a lot of minke whales in polar seas. Most other baleen whales have almost died out because of hunting.

Blue whales are the biggest animals that have ever lived. They weigh more than 30 elephants and their eyes are the size of soccer balls.

Blue whale

Callosities

Right whale

Right whales have patches of tough, white skin, called callosities, on their heads. Scientists can recognize each right whale by the pattern of its callosities.

Humpback whale

Humpback whales "talk" to each other by singing underwater. They make all kinds of whistling, rumbling and groaning noises.

Migration

Many baleen whales breed in winter in warm seas near the equator, and migrate to cold polar seas to feed during the summer. Some whales swim north to the Arctic and others swim south to the Antarctic. This map shows the migration routes of humpback whales.

ARCTIC OCEAN

EUROPE
N. AMERICA
ASIA
AFRICA
S. AMERICA
Equator
AUSTRALIA
ANTARCTICA
SOUTHERN OCEAN

Summer feeding places
Winter breeding places
→ Migration routes

Making a splash

Whales sometimes leap right out of the water and fall back in with a loud splash. This is called breaching. Nobody really knows why whales breach. It may be a way of communicating with other whales.

Humpback whale breaching

Blowing bubbles

Humpback whales sometimes make "nets" out of bubbles, to catch food. These pictures show how they do this.

The whale swims slowly to the surface in an upward spiral. As it swims, it blows air bubbles out of its blowhole.

The bubbles rise to the surface, making a circle. Krill collects in the middle of the circle.

With its mouth open, the whale bursts out of the water in the middle of the circle, and takes a huge gulp of krill.

Mothers and babies

These pictures show a mother right whale and her baby swimming along together. Baby whales are called calves.

Every now and then, the calf dives underneath its mother, so that it can feed on her milk.

When it has finished feeding, the calf makes its way back up to the surface, and continues to swim.

Toothed whales

Toothed whales eat mainly fish and squid. They often live together in groups, called pods. Members of a pod "talk" to each other in whistles and clicks. Killer whales, sperm whales, belugas and narwhals are all toothed whales found in polar seas.

Beluga whales are very "chatty". They make all kinds of mooing, chirping, squeaking, whistling and clanging noises. Beluga whales live in the Arctic.

Beluga whale

Sperm whales helping an injured member of their pod

Members of a sperm whale pod often help each other. If one whale is injured, the others make a circle around it, supporting it near the surface so it can breathe.

Narwhal

Narwhals live in the Arctic. Males, and some females, have a spiral tusk, about 7ft (2m) long, which grows forward through their upper lip.

Whale tracking

Scientists track whales to find out more about their movements. The most modern way of tracking is by satellite. A radio transmitter is attached to a whale. As the whale swims along, the transmitter sends out signals which are picked up by a satellite going around the Earth. The satellite beams the information down to a receiving station on land.

Radio transmitter attached to beluga whale

This map shows how a beluga whale in the Arctic was tracked by a satellite. The whale was tracked for almost 311 miles (500km) before its transmitter fell off.

Satellite picked up signal from radio transmitter each time it passed over whale.

Satellite beamed down information about whale's position each time it passed over receiving station.

Path of whale

Path of satellite

Radio transmitter on whale sent signals up to satellite

Tracking of whale started here

Receiving station on land

Killer whales

Killer whales are found in all seas, including polar seas. They are the fiercest whales. They eat fish, squid, birds, seals and even other whales. They usually hunt in groups and share food with each other (see page 23).

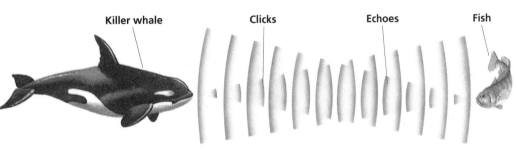

Killer whale   Clicks   Echoes   Fish

As they swim along, killer whales, and other toothed whales, make high-pitched clicking noises.

These clicks bounce off any object in their way, such as a fish, and send echoes back to the whale.

From these echoes, the whale can tell the position of the fish, and can catch it.

Blowing

Whales have to come to the surface of the sea to breathe. They blow out stale air and breathe in fresh air through a blowhole on the top of their heads. The air they blow out contains tiny drops of water, which spray upward. You can tell which species a whale is by the shape of its blow.

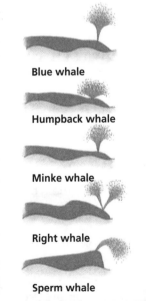

Blue whale

Humpback whale

Minke whale

Right whale

Sperm whale

Killer whales often hold themselves upright in the water, with their heads above the surface, to look around. This is called spy hopping.

Seals

Seals are mammals which live in the sea. In spring, they come on to land, or ice, to give birth to their babies, which are called pups. Seals are clumsy on land but are very good swimmers. They eat mainly fish, squid and krill. Seals are kept warm by their fur, and by a thick layer of fat under their skin. All the seals on these two pages live in the Arctic.

Harp seal pup

Harp seals are born with fluffy, white coats. Their mothers feed and take care of them for about 10 days. Then the pups grow their adult coats and must look after themselves.

Mother harp seal

Hunting seals

The Inuit people who live in the Arctic have always hunted seals for food and to make clothes from their skins. Today, there are laws protecting seals from hunting, but Inuit who still depend on seals in order to survive are allowed to hunt a small number each year. You can find out more about hunting on page 31.

Hooded seals

Hooded seals get their name because males can inflate the top part of their heads, into a kind of hood. They can also blow out the skin inside their noses, into a red balloon. They do this when they are excited or in danger.

Hooded seal with inflated hood

Hooded seal with inflated nostril

This Inuit hunter is waiting beside a hole in the ice for a seal to appear. His weapon is a traditional harpoon, but today many hunters use rifles instead.

Birth in a snow den

Ringed seals give birth to their pups in snow dens, to shelter them from the wind and to hide them from Arctic foxes and polar bears. They often make more than one den, so they can move the pup if there is danger.

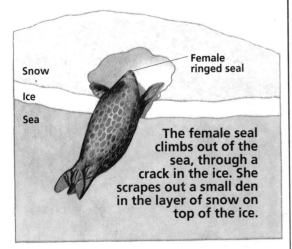

Snow

Ice

Sea

Female ringed seal

The female seal climbs out of the sea, through a crack in the ice. She scrapes out a small den in the layer of snow on top of the ice.

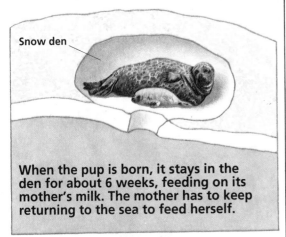

Snow den

When the pup is born, it stays in the den for about 6 weeks, feeding on its mother's milk. The mother has to keep returning to the sea to feed herself.

Arctic fox

If a fox or bear attacks and there is no time to move the pup, the mother slips back into the sea, leaving her pup behind.

Walruses

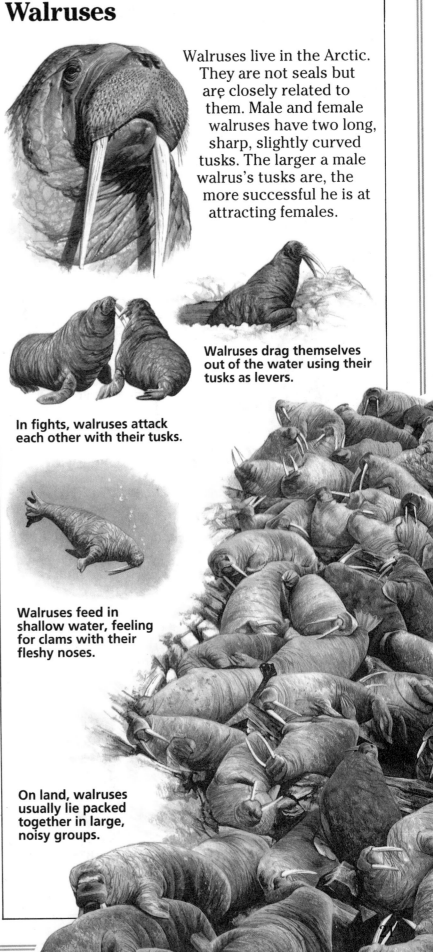

Walruses live in the Arctic. They are not seals but are closely related to them. Male and female walruses have two long, sharp, slightly curved tusks. The larger a male walrus's tusks are, the more successful he is at attracting females.

Walruses drag themselves out of the water using their tusks as levers.

In fights, walruses attack each other with their tusks.

Walruses feed in shallow water, feeling for clams with their fleshy noses.

On land, walruses usually lie packed together in large, noisy groups.

Eared seals and true seals

Eared seal

True seal

There are two main types of seals - those with ears (eared seals) and those without (true seals). Eared seals can turn their back flippers forward to help them waddle along on land. True seals cannot do this. They drag themselves along using their front flippers. Apart from Antarctic fur seals, all the seals in this book are true seals. The seals on these two pages live in the Antarctic.

Crabeater seals on ice floe

There are more crabeater seals than all the other seals in the world added together - over 15 million of them. In spite of their name, they eat krill, not crabs.

In the 1950s, there were only a few hundred Antarctic fur seals left, because of hunting. They were in danger of dying out. Today, these seals are protected by law and there are about one-and-a-half million of them.

Antarctic fur seal

Leopard seals have huge heads and sharp, saw-like teeth. They are the only seals which eat other kinds of seals, but their main food is penguins (see page 11).

Leopard seal's head

Living underwater

Seals are very well adapted to living underwater. Their bodies are a good shape and they have webbed flippers to help them swim. Weddell seals spend the whole winter in the sea, under the ice shelves around Antarctica. They have to come to the surface for air because, like whales, seals cannot breathe underwater.

Weddell seals make breathing holes in the ice, where they can come to the surface for air.

The seals keep their breathing holes open by scraping at the ice with their teeth.

Weddell seals can dive as deep as 875yds (800m) and stay underwater for an hour without coming up to breathe.

Weddell seal

Elephant seals

Elephant seals are the world's biggest seals. They get their name because the adult males have a loose, wrinkled piece of skin above their noses, which they can inflate into a kind of trunk. At breeding times, thousands of elephant seals gather in huge groups on beaches on islands around Antarctica. Pairs of males have long, fierce fights over females. The seal which is older and bigger usually wins.

Elephant seals fighting

When two elephant seals fight, they face each other, stretch their heads upward and roar loudly. Then they attack each other's necks with their teeth. They have thick skin on their necks to protect them.

The three small pictures below show how elephant seals' noses grow. The seals cannot inflate their noses into trunks until they are about eight years old.

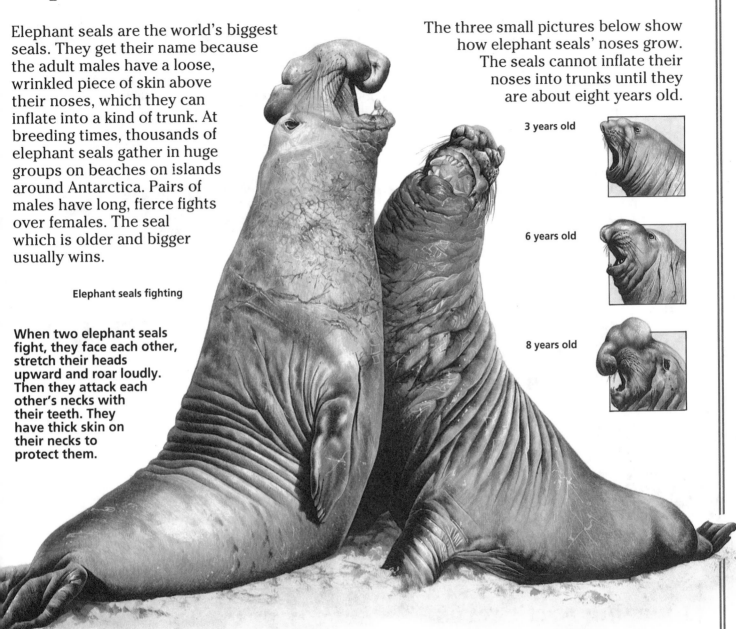

3 years old

6 years old

8 years old

Danger from killer whales

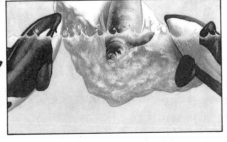

Killer whales eat all kinds of seals. Here, a group of killer whales has found a crabeater seal asleep on an ice floe. The whales move in and surround the floe.

One whale leans on the edge of the floe, using its weight to push the floe downward. Another whale pushes the floe upward from the other side. The seal begins to slip.

As the floe tilts, the seal slides off, straight into the jaws of one of the killer whales. The other whales will swim up to take their share of the food.

Arctic birds

Each spring, thousands of birds migrate to the Arctic, to feed and breed there during the summer. All kinds of food, such as plants and insects, are uncovered when the ice melts (see pages 28-29). In autumn, most birds leave to spend the winter in warmer places. Here are some of the birds that spend the summer in the Arctic.

Arctic skua

Fulmar

Arctic redpoll

Snow bunting

Glaucous gull

Rough-legged buzzard

Turnstone

Golden plover

Red-necked phalarope

Red-legged kittiwake

Gyrfalcon

Siberian white crane

Black-throated diver

Little auk

Long-tailed duck

Harlequin duck

Barnacle goose

Bewick swan

White-fronted goose

Snow goose

Brent goose

Amazing Arctic terns

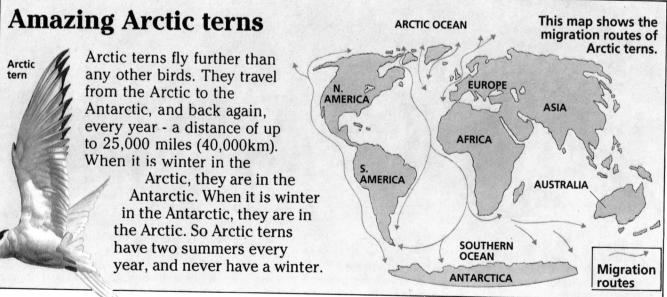

Arctic tern

Arctic terns fly further than any other birds. They travel from the Arctic to the Antarctic, and back again, every year - a distance of up to 25,000 miles (40,000km). When it is winter in the Arctic, they are in the Antarctic. When it is winter in the Antarctic, they are in the Arctic. So Arctic terns have two summers every year, and never have a winter.

This map shows the migration routes of Arctic terns.

ARCTIC OCEAN

N. AMERICA

EUROPE

ASIA

AFRICA

S. AMERICA

AUSTRALIA

SOUTHERN OCEAN

ANTARCTICA

Migration routes

24

Staying for the winter

Snowy owls, ptarmigans and ravens stay on the Arctic tundra all through the winter. They have to survive the cold, find food for themselves and their chicks, and avoid being eaten by enemies, such as Arctic foxes.

Snowy owl with chicks

Snowy owls nest on the ground, usually on slightly raised areas, so they can keep a look-out for enemies. They do not lay all their eggs at once, so there may be chicks of different sizes in the nest. The adults bring lemmings for the chicks to feed on.

Ptarmigan in summer

Ptarmigans dig plants out of the snow with their feet. In winter, they are white, to blend with the snow. In summer, they are patchy brown, to blend with rocks and plants.

Ptarmigan in winter

Ravens are black all year long, so they do not blend with their background in summer or winter. They have few enemies, though, because they are so strong and fierce.

Raven

Nests on cliffs

Many Arctic birds lay their eggs on cliffs so enemies on the ground cannot reach them. They breed in large groups, called colonies. This picture shows some of the birds you might see nesting together on a cliff.

Puffins nest in burrows which they hollow out in the soil near the top of cliffs.

Puffins

Kittiwakes make messy nests on narrow cliff ledges.

Kittiwakes

Guillemots lay their eggs on bare ledges. The eggs are pointed at one end so that if they are knocked, they roll around in a circle, instead of forward off the ledge.

Guillemots

Guillemot egg

Razorbills lay their eggs on ledges under overhanging rocks.

Razorbills

Antarctic birds

Many types of birds live in the Antarctic as well as penguins. Penguins cannot fly, but most other Antarctic birds spend their lives flying over the stormy Southern Ocean, feeding on fish, squid and krill. They only come on to land to breed. The most common Antarctic birds are penguins, petrels and albatrosses.

Albatrosses

Albatrosses are the largest sea birds in the world. They also live longer than most other birds - it is quite common for albatrosses to live for 30 years and some live for 70 or 80 years. Four species of albatrosses breed in the Antarctic. They usually breed in large colonies, with thousands of nests together.

Wandering albatross

Wandering albatrosses can travel as far as 2,330 miles (3,750km) in one day. They use their long, narrow wings to glide along on air currents.

Wandering albatrosses have longer wings than any other bird. The distance from the tip of one wing to the tip of the other can be as much as 11.5ft (3.5m). This means each wing is about the length of a person.

Gray-headed albatross chick on nest

Albatrosses make raised nests out of mud, grass and moss. They hollow out the top, line it with grass and feathers and lay a single egg inside. When the chick hatches, it sits on top of the nest.

Finding a partner

Albatrosses take a long time to find a partner, but it is something that most of them only have to do once. Pairs of albatrosses usually stay together for their whole lives. These pictures show how a pair gets together.

The male attracts females by doing a courtship display. He points his beak upward, holds out his wings and whistles.

When a female arrives, the two dance face to face. They stretch out their wings and snap their beaks loudly.

When they have paired up, the birds sit side by side on the nest area, nibbling at each other's necks and calling softly.

Diving for fish

Blue-eyed shags swim along on the surface of the sea and dive to the bottom to catch fish.

They swim back up to the surface with the fish, eat it and then dive again immediately.

After 2 or 3 dives, they often stand on a rock and hold their wings out to dry.

Petrels

Petrels are related to albatrosses. There are 18 different species living in the Antarctic. Here are three of them.

Snow petrels hover over the pack ice around Antarctica. They dive down between the ice floes to snatch krill out of the water.

Snow petrel

Giant petrels are the largest petrels. They have enormous beaks which look as if they are made up of lots of pieces.

Giant petrel

Storm petrels flutter along just above the surface of the sea, with their legs dangling down. They look as if they are walking on the water.

Wilson's storm petrel

Chick snatchers

Large, fierce birds, called skuas, sometimes snatch and eat the chicks of other birds, such as penguins. They wait around near penguin rookeries until they see a chick which has wandered away from the crèche. Then they rush in and snatch it. Skuas also steal penguin eggs which have been left unguarded.

This gentoo penguin is trying to stop a skua from snatching her chick.

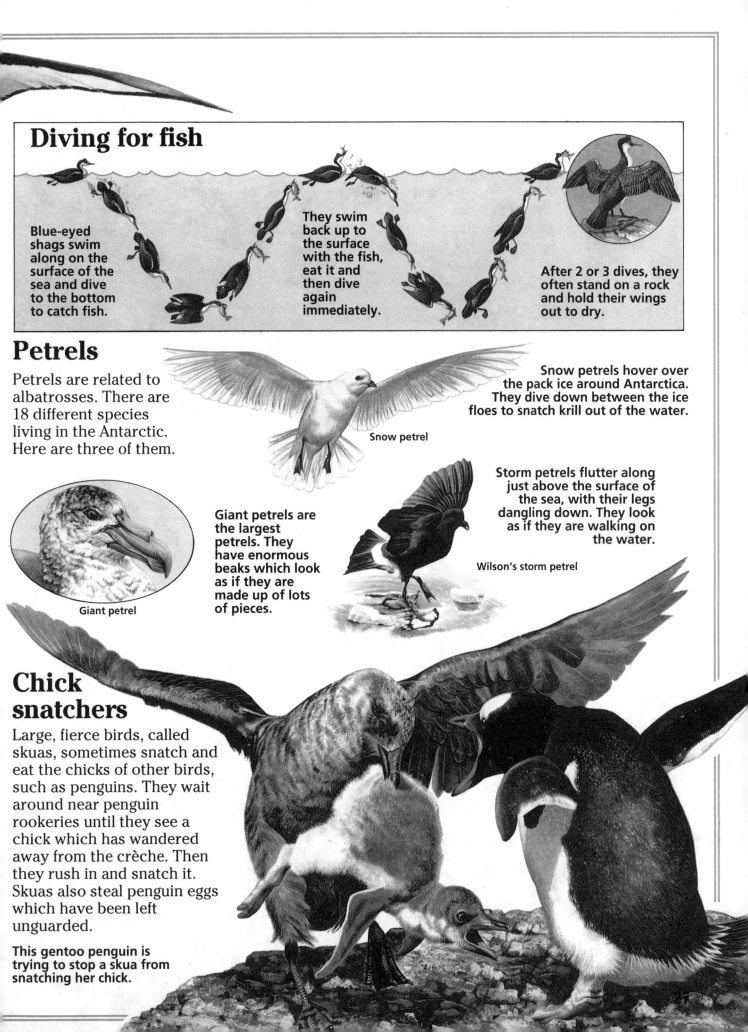

Summer in the Arctic

During summer in the Arctic, some of the ice on the tundra melts. Plants grow, insects hatch and lemmings come out of their burrows. This means there is suddenly plenty of food, both for animals which have spent all winter on the tundra, and for those which arrive just for the summer. They can even feed all night because in the Arctic the sun never sets in summer. The summer is short, though - after six to eight weeks, the ground freezes and winter begins again.

Lichens

Mosses

Mosses and lichens are the most common Arctic plants. Lichens grow very slowly and may take hundreds of years to grow an inch (about 3cm).

Flowering plants

It is hard for plants to grow in the Arctic. Even in summer, it is cold and windy. In winter, there is no sunshine and all the water is frozen into ice. When the ice does melt, the soil is often flooded. Despite all this, over a thousand species of flowering plants grow on the tundra. Here are some of them.

Arctic poppy

Moss campion

Campanulas

Purple saxifrage

Yellow avens

Buttercups

Diapensia

Yellow mountain saxifrage

Arctic azalea

Flocks of birds arrive to feed on plants and insects, and to raise their chicks. The chicks have to grow quickly so they can fly back to warmer places before the Arctic winter begins.

Flock of snow geese

Arctic poppies

Purple saxifrage

In summer, caribou and other mammals are pestered by biting insects, such as mosquitoes and blackflies. Millions of insects hatch out of their eggs which have been frozen in ponds and lakes all winter.

Cotton grass

Tundra food web

This food web shows who eats what on the Arctic tundra. For example, lemmings eat plants, and are eaten by skuas, snowy owls, Arctic foxes and stoats. (The pictures are not to scale.)

Skuas

Snowy owls

Arctic foxes

Wolves

Stoats

Hares

Musk oxen

Caribou

Lemmings

Ptarmigans

Plants

Boggy tundra

The ice on the surface of the tundra melts in summer, but about 1m (3ft) below is a thick layer of ice, called permafrost, which never melts. Water cannot drain through the permafrost, so it stays on the tundra, in bogs and ponds.

Permafrost

Chilly Antarctic

Antarctica is much colder than the Arctic tundra. Even in summer, most of the land is covered with ice. On the outer edges of Antarctica, there are mosses, lichens, two species of flowering plants and a few insects.

People in polar lands

People, such as the Inuit and the Sami, have been living in the Arctic for thousands of years, without harming their environment. When outsiders came to the Arctic, and later to the Antarctic, they were not so careful, as you can find out on page 31.

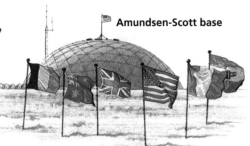
Amundsen-Scott base

Nobody lives in the Antarctic, but scientists from many countries spend time there, learning about the place and its wildlife. The US scientific base near the South Pole is called Amundsen-Scott.

The Inuit

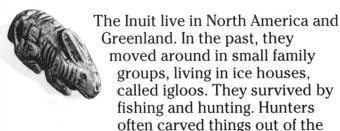

The Inuit live in North America and Greenland. In the past, they moved around in small family groups, living in ice houses, called igloos. They survived by fishing and hunting. Hunters often carved things out of the tusks and bones of the animals that they killed. Today, many Inuit stay in one place instead of moving around. They live in houses in towns and go to work every day.

Inuit still build igloos to spend the night in when they go on hunting trips. Igloos are made from blocks of ice. The cracks are filled in with loose snow.

The Sami

The Sami people of Scandinavia and Russia used to survive by keeping herds of reindeer. They got meat and milk from them, and used their skins to make clothes, and tents to live in. They also used the reindeer to carry loads and to pull sleighs. Some Sami still live in this way today, but, like the Inuit, many have given up their old way of life and now live and work in towns instead.

Sami tent made from reindeer skins

This brightly dressed Sami woman is a reindeer-herder. Many herders travel along the reindeer migration routes, stopping whenever the reindeer stop to feed.

Polar explorers

In 1909, Robert Peary became the first person to reach the North Pole. The first person to reach the South Pole was Roald Amundsen. He got there on 14th December 1911, beating another explorer, Robert Falcon Scott, by just 35 days. Scott and all his companions died on their way back.

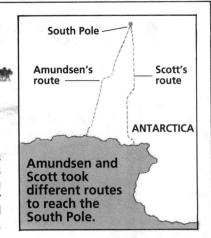

South Pole

Amundsen's route

Scott's route

ANTARCTICA

Amundsen and Scott took different routes to reach the South Pole.

Explorers struggled across the ice in freezing temperatures and bitter winds. Teams of dogs pulled sledges piled with food and equipment.

Hunting

Outsiders did not hunt for their own survival, but sold huge numbers of animal skins for money. Polar bears, musk oxen and many species of seals and whales almost died out in some areas. Today, most species are protected.

In the Canadian Arctic, thousands of baby harp seals used to be killed every year for their fur. Today, very few are killed because fewer people want to wear fur coats.

Fishing

Since the 1970s, people have been catching large amounts of fish, squid and krill. If numbers of these get too low, the animals which eat them, such as seals and whales, will suffer too. This can be stopped if people agree to limit how much they catch.

Modern fishing boats can catch huge amounts at one time. Animals, such as sea birds and seals, can get caught in the nets by mistake.

Pollution

Polar areas are not as polluted as other places, because they are far away from big groups of people. In the Arctic, though, oil pollution is a problem. For example, in 1989, off the coast of Alaska, USA, a lot of oil spilled into the sea from the Exxon Valdez tanker. In cold water, oil takes years to break up and disappear.

If sea birds swallow oil, they are poisoned. They can also die of cold if oil clogs their feathers.

The ozone layer

In the Earth's atmosphere, a layer of gas, called ozone, protects plants and animals from the sun's harmful rays. In 1982, scientists discovered that the ozone layer above Antarctica was very thin. They believe it is being destroyed by gases, called CFCs, which come from things such as refrigerators and aerosols.

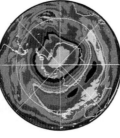

This satellite picture shows the thinning, or "hole", in the ozone layer above Antarctica. The hole is the orange part in the middle.

Building

In the Arctic, people mine for oil, coal, and so on. Mining, fishing and hunting lead to the building of roads, mines, ports, pipelines and airstrips (places for planes to land). This changes the environment and can disturb wildlife.

In Antarctica, penguins' breeding areas have been dug up to build airstrips. The environmental group, Greenpeace, has been trying to stop this from happening.

Peace for polar lands

So far, 40 countries have agreed to protect Antarctica. In 1991, they decided that no mining would be allowed for 50 years. Conservation groups also work to protect polar lands. The Arctic and the Antarctic have not yet been spoiled like so many other places. It is not too late to keep them like this, so plants, animals and people can go on living there in peace.

Tourists can only visit Antarctica on carefully organized trips, so animals, such as these albatrosses, are not disturbed too much.

Index

Photograph on page 5, © WWF/Thor Larsen.
Satellite photograph of ozone hole on page 31, courtesy of NASA.
All other photographs, © Bryan & Cherry Alexander

ISBN 0-590-48048-0
Copyright © 1992 by Usborne Publishing Ltd. All rights reserved. Published by Scholastic Inc., 555 Broadway, New York, NY 10012, by arrangement with Usborne Publishing Ltd.
12 11 10 9 8